SANSKRIT LINGUISTICS AND ITS APPLICATIONS TO UNDERSTANDING THE UNIVERSE

UNIVERSE MODELLING, DIGITAL TWIN, ONE'S SCIENTIFIC IDENTITY AND KARMA

NISHANTH MEHANATHAN

I dedicate this book to my family, friends, teachers, Shree *Krishna, Shani Bhagawan* and *Vaishnodevi Ma*

Contents

Acknowledgements

I would like to thank all my teachers, friends, colleagues and family members for the warm support they have extended to me while working on this book, these were the giants on whose shoulders I stood.

The theme of this book has evolved over the past 2 decades. The search for the structure within the universe has been my passion since I started studying science as it would encompass all fields, hence I would be able to absorb knowledge from any field I came across into an understandable model. Universe modelling was what I wanted to do since my teens, the inspiration came to me from the game "Age of Empires" which had modelled a miniature version of an ancient world with various empires interacting with one another. I wondered if it was possible to model any arbitrary collection of objects like nations, economies, software systems and so on. And the work presented in this book is an answer to that problem. I would like to thank God who helped me in this journey and gave me this opportunity to solve this problem.

Introduction

In this book, we discuss Sanskrit linguistics, its advances over modern-day English linguistics and its application to Universe modelling. The topics covered include:

1. Verbal knowledge representation as a network of relations.
2. Creation of the model (verbal model) of an object/thing or System of objects/things for any field of science or study. It resolves a body of knowledge into a world of its own.
3. Resolving the model further (graphical model) so that the objects/system of objects can be represented in a visual/graphical manner on computers like a virtual world. This resolved digital twin of an object or system of objects is similar to how one would perceive them in a real-world so that it can be represented graphically.

The technical topics covered include:

1. Sentence meaning and the definition of a sentence
2. What is an object or thing?
3. Classification of words in a language and word meaning
4. Action and its accomplishers
5. Classification of actions
6. Theory of nouns and verbs

Also discussed are other important non-technical topics:

1. One's true scientific identity and oneness with all living creatures
2. The theory of Karma or action and the consequences of action

The discussion is based on the viewpoint of Sanskrit linguists and their ideas about a thing or system of things. It reflects their understanding of a thing which is profound and well understood as Sanskrit is one of the oldest languages known to mankind (~5000 years).

A "Universe Model" essentially behaves like a system or collection of objects it models ("Universe"). All the fields of knowledge can be said to be knowledge about objects or system of objects, hence this modelling theory is applicable across all fields of knowledge. Another theory which simplifies the model and permits the easy graphical representation of the model is also presented.

The study of these technical topics surprisingly leads to an understanding of self, the universe and one's actions.

Technical section

Sentence meaning and theory of sentences, classification of words in a language and word meaning, action and its accomplishers, classification of actions, theory of nouns and verbs, what is an object or thing, universe modelling and the digital twin

CHAPTER ONE

VERBAL TESTIMONY

Knowledge is obtained in various ways. In the Indian philosophy there are three main means of obtaining valid knowledge as enumerated in Figure 1:

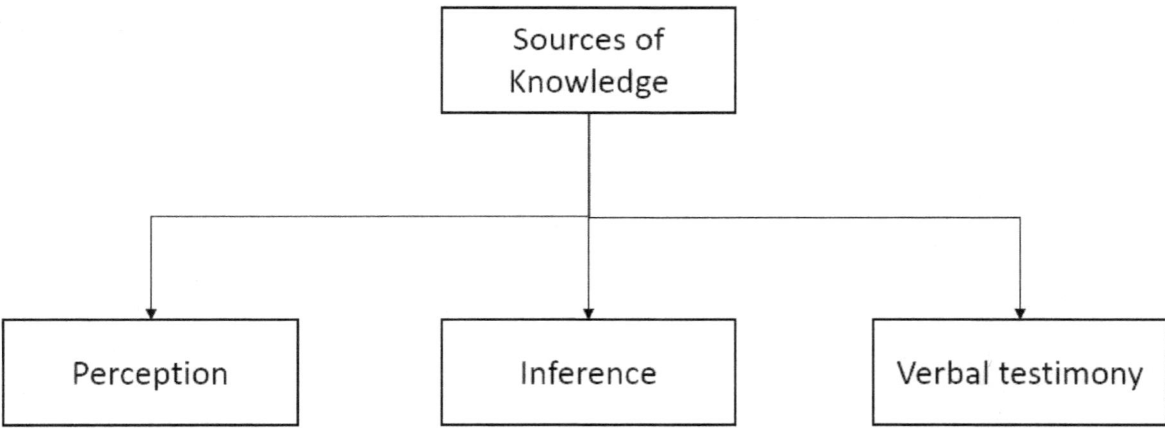

Figure 1. While an object undergoes changes, the identity is the "unchanging"; the "unchanging" is the reason for us recognizing the object or it still being the object.

1. Perception (*pratyaksha*)
2. Inference (*anumana*)
3. Verbal testimony (*shabda*)

The purpose of "verbal testimony" is to exchange knowledge, especially between individuals or knowledge from an expert to a person seeking knowledge. It is either through the written or the spoken medium.

Exchange of knowledge between individuals:
In Indian philosophy the means of exchanging knowledge about something between two individuals is called "word" or "*shabda*" and it is defined as "*apta vakya*" [1], which is translated as a true sentence or sentence in general from a reliable source. The reliable source is the highest authority. A sentence is defined as a collection of words grammatically related to one another and a word is defined as that which has the power to convey a meaning or indicate an object [2]. In this system, the knowledge occurs as a sentence. The purpose of a reliable source is that the knowledge is true and the sentences are valid.

A sentence by itself without apprehension of the word meanings is of no purpose. When the words and their meaning are apprehended and associated we gain knowledge (sentence meaning). The reliable source conveys the sentence but acquiring knowledge (sentence meaning) from the sentences is another task in itself. So successful transfer of knowledge is a two-step process:

Step 1: Converting one's knowledge to testimony or account.

Step 2: Obtaining knowledge from the account or testimony and grasping the meaning of sentences constituting the testimony.

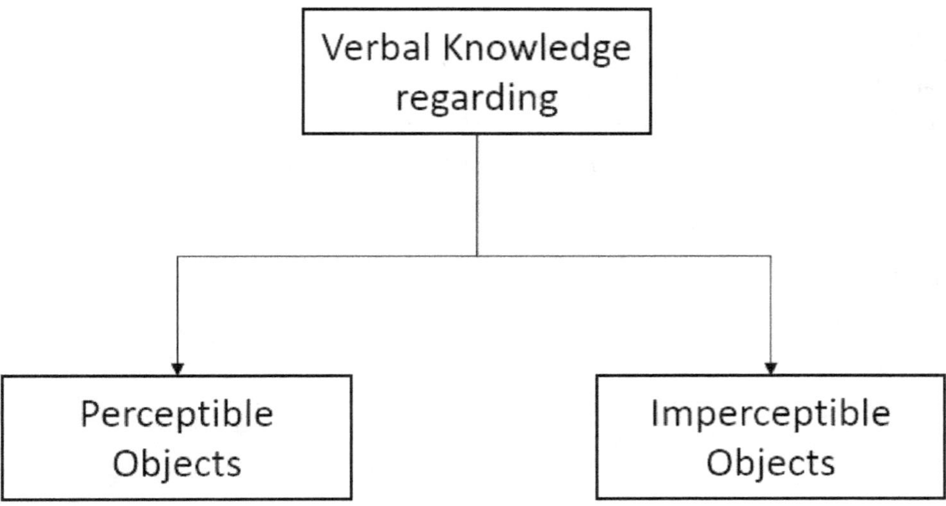

Figure 2. Verbal knowledge is regarding perceptible objects or imperceptible objects

Verbal knowledge is of two types [3] as shown in Figure 2:

1. That relating to perceptible objects
2. That relating to imperceptible objects

So from a Digital Twin point of view, the world of objects can be perceptible or imperceptible. Therefore, all the knowledge we have about a thing is nothing but a collection of sentences.

Knowledge of thing | What a thing is: {S1, S2, S3}
Where S1, S2, and S3 are sentences describing the thing.

Notes

1. आप्तवाक्यं शब्दः (*āptavākyaṃ śabdaḥ*) Tarka. Sangrah. पृ 182.
2. Chandradhar Sharma, *A Critical Survey of Indian Philosophy*, Page 204
3. Satischandra Chatterjee, *The Nyaya Theory of Knowledge: A Critical Study Some Problems of Logic and Metaphysics*, Page 318, Nyaya sutra 1.1.8

CHAPTER TWO

SANSKRIT SENTENCES AND SIMILARITIES OBSERVED IN ENGLISH

In Sanskrit linguistics, a sentence is recognized as a group of words syntactically connected [1]. The grammarian Yaska posits that the verb is the vital unit of language through which we express our intentions and actions and a sentence without a verb serves no purpose [2].

Patanjali defines a sentence as "*akhyata savisesnam*" [3], a finite verb with qualifying word(s). *Bhartrhari* in his *Vakyapadiya* states that "*akhyatasabdah*" which means that the verb is the sentence[3], an action expressed by a verb is sentential-meaning (*Kriya-vakyartha*)[4].

According to *Patanjali*: A sentence is a verb with qualifying words and the action expressed by the verb is sentential-meaning. The qualificand of any sentence is an action or *kriya* denoted by a verb, qualified as being brought about by different participants. The Sanskrit sentence structure is depicted in Figure 1.

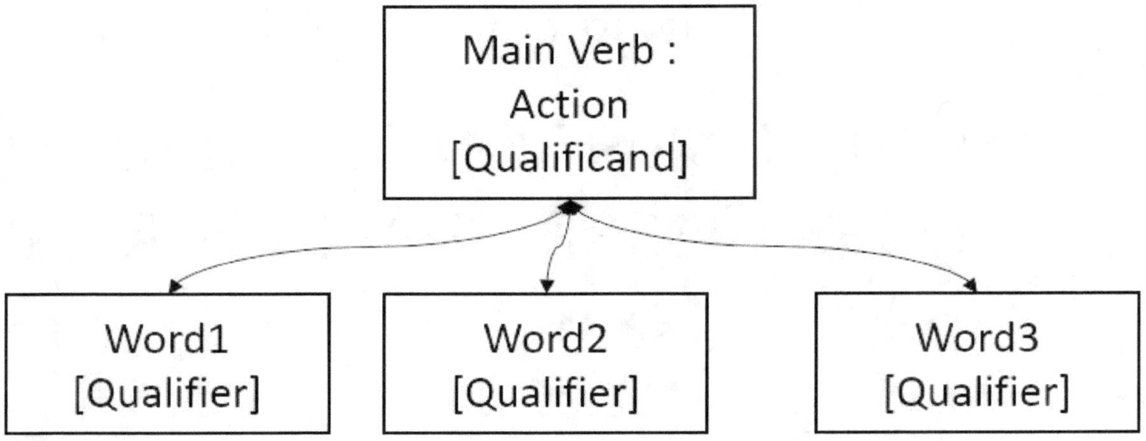

Figure 1. Sentence structure in Sanskrit a verb qualified directly and indirectly by other words

The English language seems to follow a similar pattern under certain conditions. Let us explore how and when:

Modern dependency grammar

1. Modern Dependency grammar was created by the French linguist Lucien Tesniere; however, there is another view that it goes back to the middle ages. Dependency grammar revolves around the observation that in a sentence all but one word depends on other words. This independent word is called the root word and is termed the central or main element. [5]
2. The structure of a sentence is described in terms of a set of binary relations that are observed between the words in a sentence. [6]
3. The relations in a dependency structure capture the head-dependent relationship between the words in a sentence. [6]
4. Dependency parsing identifies a root word (often the main verb) and then describes the other words with respect to that word and to each other.
5. The dependency structure is a tree which has a main verb as its root (head) or central element.

6. Whenever two words are connected by a dependency relation, we are saying that one of them is the head and the other is the dependent and that there is a link connecting them. In general, the dependent is the modifier, object, or complement; the head plays a larger role in determining the behaviour of the pair.
7. Except for the main verb, all words depend on other words. The main verb is considered the root of the dependency structure.
8. In most cases, the root of a dependency tree is the main verb of the sentence.
9. And the structure of a sentence is described in terms of a set of binary relations that are observed between the words in a sentence.

Sentence theorem

From the above analysis, the following can be posited about the sentence:

The sentence is the main verb and its qualifiers (when the root of a sentence is the main verb) where the words directly/indirectly qualify the main verb.

This is the Sentence theorem in short applicable to the English language. The words in a sentence have relations both direct and indirect with the main verb, and the relation provides the differentiation to the main verb or qualifies it. So the main verb behaves as the qualificand and the other words as its qualifiers[direct and indirect].

Diagram clarifying the sentence theorem.

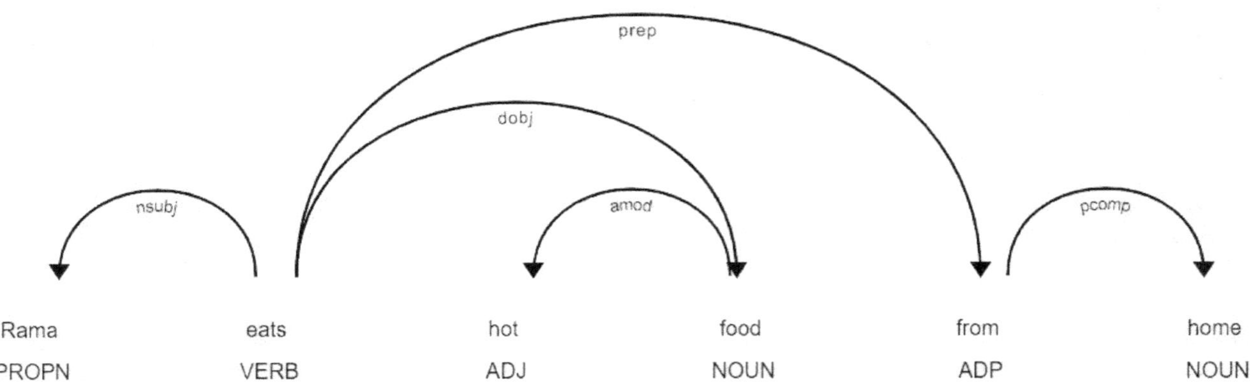

Figure 2. Dependency tree of a sentence

In the above figure, Rama, food and from have direct relation (qualify eats directly) with the main verb and hot and home have indirect relation (qualify eats indirectly).

Relations with the main verb. These words qualify, directly and indirectly, the main verb eats.

- Every sentence has two parts: a subject and a predicate. A predicate is the part of a sentence or a clause, that tells what the agent or subject is doing or what the agent or subject is.
- In essence, a sentence conveys the action a subject is performing.
- The sentence meaning is an action performed by the subject.
- What is conveyed or indicated is the meaning of that entity

Notes

1. Nyaya, *Encyclopedia of Indian philosophies* Volume 5, Karl H Potter, Page. 26

2. *Tad.yatra.ubhe.bhāva.pradhāne.bhavataḥ* – Nir. l. 1

3. Bhatta, V. P. "*SENTENCE (VĀKYA) AND SENTENCE MEANING (VĀKYĀRTHA).*" Annals of the Bhandarkar Oriental Research Institute, vol. 92, 2011, pp. 27–43. JSTOR, http://www.jstor.org/stable/43941270. Accessed 24 May 2022.

4. Gajjam, Jayashree & Kanojia, Diptesh & Kulkarni, Malhar. (2018). *New Vistas to study Bhartrhari:* Cognitive NLP.

5. *A Fundamental Algorithm for Dependency* Parsing Michael A. Covington

6. *Speech and Language Processing.* Daniel Jurafsky & James H. Martin. Copyright © 2021. All rights reserved. Draft of December 29, 2021.

CHAPTER THREE

WHAT IS AN OBJECT?

An object is defined as the substratum of the genus, differentia and action, or that which has attributes [1] as depicted in Figure 1.

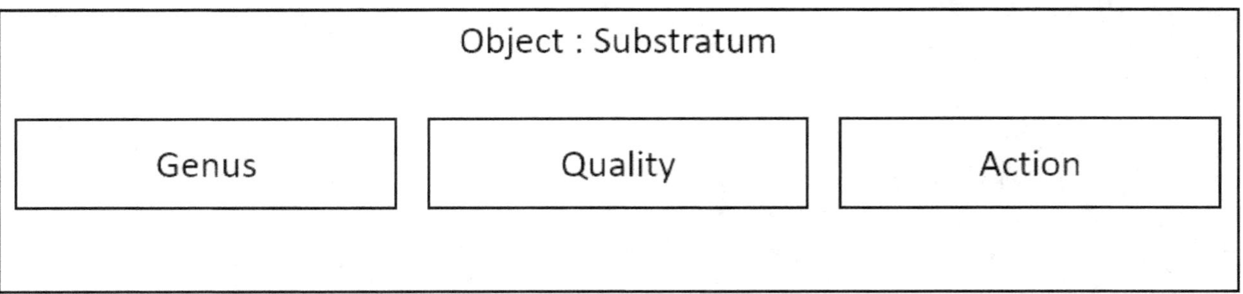

Figure1. Object as the substratum of genus, differentia and action

These attributes are further classified as shown in Figure 2. An attribute is of two types- one that is inherent and another which is imposed upon it like a name. The inherent attribute again is of two kinds, an attribute that is fully accomplished and that which is in the process of accomplishment. An accomplished attribute is of two types- the life-giving genus or class and the quality. Genus is never found dissociated from the individuals in which it resides, while a quality serves to distinguish a thing from other things belonging to the same genus. A genus cannot dissociate from the object in which it is found.

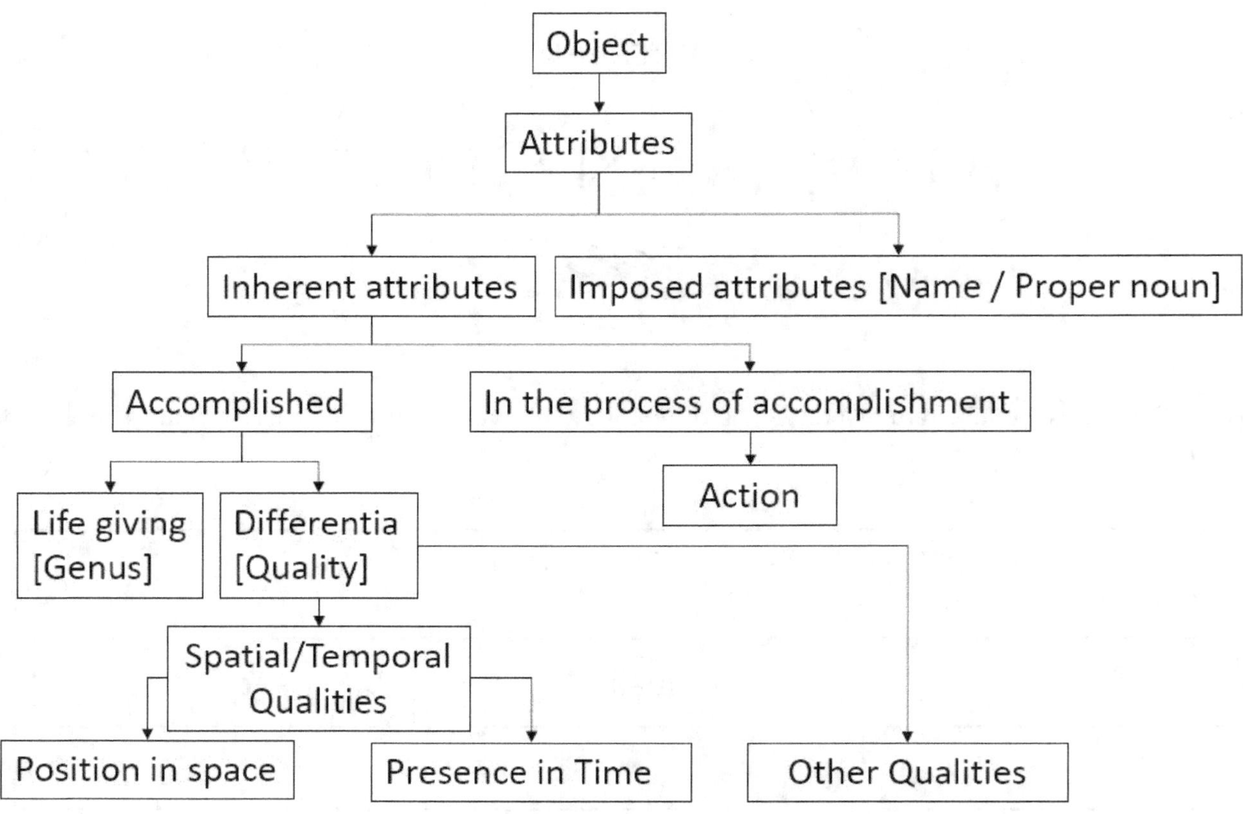

Figure 2. Object attributes, which uniquely identify an object

An example of the genus is cowness, quality is whiteness and action is cooking. An attribute of an object in process of accomplishment is called action. For instance, the colour of a cloth (brownness) is an accomplished fact. But action implies a series of activities some completed and some in the process of completion, which occupies successive portions of time.[2].

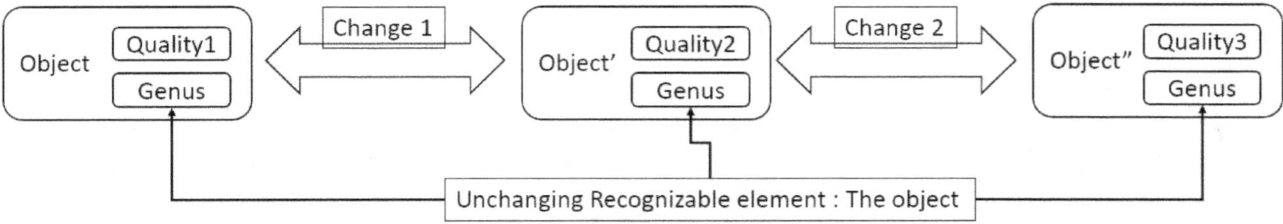

Figure 3. The unchanging recognizable element which remains across various changes

Object, its identity and the identity theorem:

Identity theorem: An object stands for that unchanging recognizable element which persists in all the changes that it undergoes [3] as shown in Figure 3. This is because if an object changes, it still remains the object hence the object is something which persists across the change and which we know to be the genus or universal.

For example, if a brass bangle (or a brass object) is twisted out of shape what remains is it being made of brass and it is an object. So it is still a brass object but the brass bangle is destroyed, we can say a brass object has changed and a brass bangle is destroyed. So speaking practically it is the genus which the object is. Qualities are properties which undergo a change. As a result of the genus persisting you are able to identify the object across all changes as the genus remains constant.

Notes

1. Charudev Shastri, *Vyakaran Mahabhashya* (*Pratham Aahrikantri*) – Page 3.
2. *Sahitya Darpan*, II.4, page 43.
3. *Vakyapadiyam of Bhartrhari*, III.1.11, III.1.12 commentary.

CHAPTER FOUR

CLASSIFICATION OF WORDS IN SANSKRIT

The Sanskrit linguists hold that the import of words is either genus, quality, action or names. Hence there are four main types of words- genus word, quality word, action word and name word [1]. It is specific to the Sanskrit language but the import or idea is universal to all languages. What is indicated by a word is of four types- genus, quality, action and proper names. Their definitions have already been given in Chapter 3. Whatever conveys anything other than a proper name, genus or action signifies a quality. These four-word types come under nouns in Sanskrit and are names for genus, action, proper name and quality.

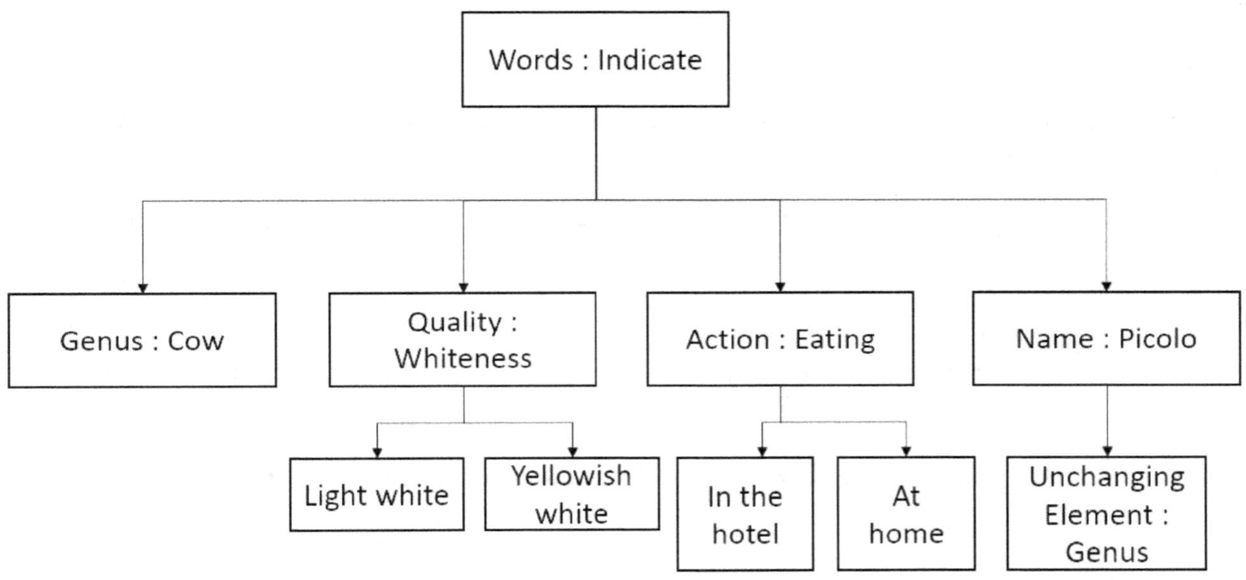

Figure 1. Types of words and what they indicate with examples.

- The linguists conclude that all four types of words refer to a genus only. This can be proved as follows. The genus word indicates a genus by itself, the quality word for example blueness is a genus on the basis of which there is a common awareness of blueness(amongst light blue, dark blue etc.). Names also signify a genus as they are spoken differently by different people and refer to the genus present in the object which is unchanging amongst changes. So all four-word categories imply genus. So the meaning of a word is a genus [2]. The classification of words and examples for each have been enumerated in Figure 1.

The individual and genus:

- That element in objects which is peculiar to them, which comes and goes is called the individual or as discussed before the quality. It is impermanent and not to be found in all objects of the class. It is relatively unreal.

- That which is permanent and which constitutes the pervading essence of an object is called the universal or genus. It is real. The individual and genus across changes have been depicted in Figure 2.

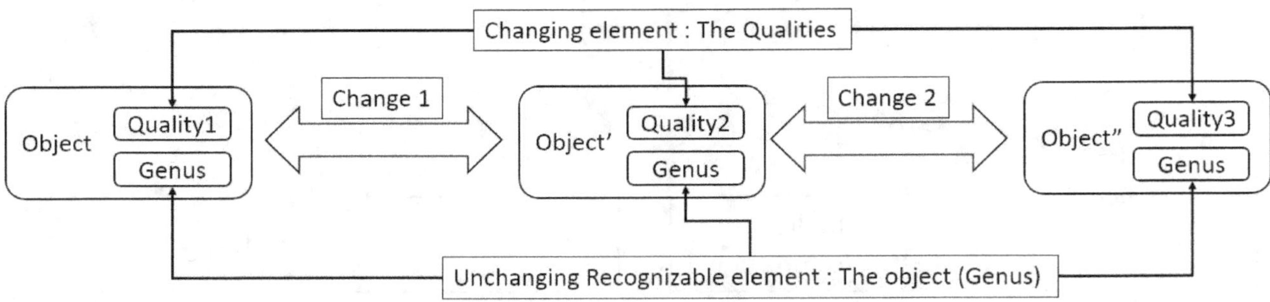

Figure 2. The Individual and the genus across the various changes.

- An example is silver ornaments such as bangles, and earrings. The shape of the ornament is impermanent as they are re-made whereas the material or silver is the persisting essence of these ornaments.
- If we go on seeking higher universals of an object we will come to what is called *Brahman* (which means what is everywhere and in everything). This is the highest universal. It is called "*mahasatta*" and is translated in English as "absolute being" or "absolute existence" [3][4].
- It is this "absolute existence" or "absolute being" found in all objects as their highest universal. As "tree-ness" is in a tree. Tree-ness is nothing but "absolute being" as it exists in a tree.
- All words express this "absolute being" / "being" and it appears in each object as their genus(for example as sand-ness in sand).
- It is Being which is differentiated according to the object in which it is present is called the universal. All words are based on it.
- The universal common to all things are ("*satta*": being):
- In all things is the comprehensive universal called 'Being'. Even non-existent things have it, as they occur in our minds. Both an action(eating) and a thing(moon) are only manifestations of being(*satta*) [5].
- A verb expresses this "being" as a process. Action is something which has processes arranged in sequence and depends upon the instrumental cause for its accomplishment. This is the universal action, a manifestation of *satta* or "Being" [6].

- The next manifestation of being is a thing. It is accomplished and is thought of as a finished thing. Like a silver ornament etc [7].
- *"Brahman* is the unchanging among changing things" which is the genus [8]. Persistence or permanence is supposed to be the test of reality/existence, we find it is only the genus that is real, for only that is unchanging while the particular or unreal changes.
- Figure 3 indicates the existence/being in all things and actions.

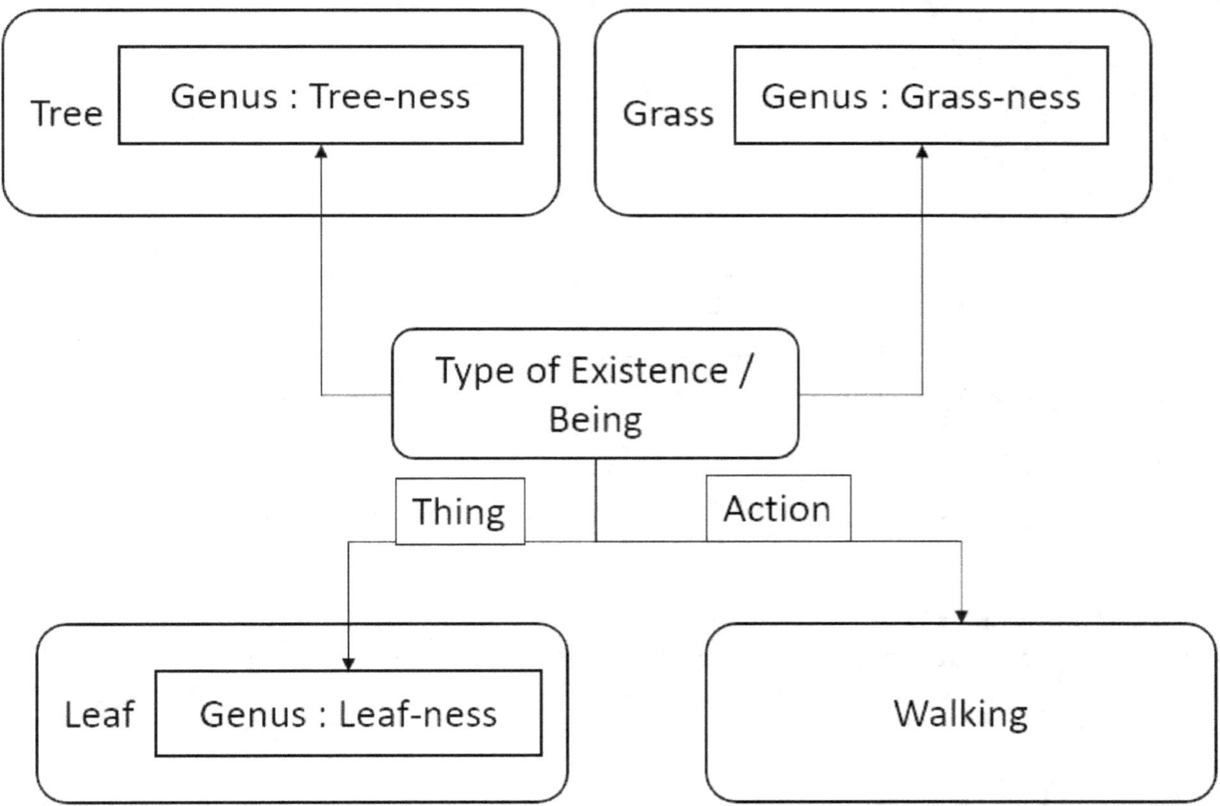

Figure 3. The Existence/Being in all things and actionption

The four types of words and determinate knowledge:
Knowledge is first obtained through perception. There are two kinds of knowledge:

1. *Nirvikalpa* **(indeterminate knowledge):** When an object is perceived without being able to know its features.
2. *Savikalpa* **(determinate knowledge):** When an object is known or we know its features. In this knowledge, there are three entities qualificand, qualifier and the relation between them. The knowledge of the qualificand, its qualifier and the relation between them is called determinate knowledge [9].

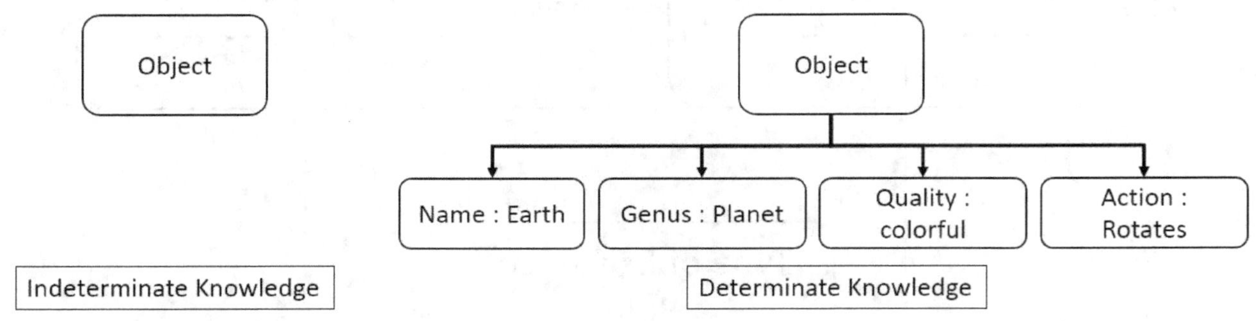

Figure 4. Two steps of perception, indeterminate and determinate

The *Naiyyayika* have determined two steps in perception, They are as shown in Figure 4.
The *Naiyyayika* maintains two types or steps in perception. The first is called *nirvikalpa* (indeterminate), when an object is perceived without being able to know its features, and the second *savikalpa* (determinate), when one is able to clearly know an object.

In *savikalpa*/determinate knowledge the following features are cognized [10]:

1. Name.
2. Genus.
3. Quality.
4. Action.

These are represented by the four categories of words, this is depicted in Figure 4.

Notes

1. Makkhanalāla Śarmā, *Bhāratīya kāvyaśāstra ke siddhānta* - Page 69.
2. Kapiladeva Dvivedī, *Arthavijñāna aura vyākaraṇadarśana* - Page 231.
3. https://www.wisdomlib.org/definition/mahasatta
4. *Vakyapadiyam* of Bhartrhari, III.1.34 commentary.
5. *Vakyapadiyam* of Bhartrhari, III.1.34 commentary.
6. *Vakyapadiyam* of Bhartrhari, III.1.35 commentary.
7. *Vakyapadiyam* of Bhartrhari, III.1.35 commentary.
8. De Beer, W.A., From Logos to Bios: Hellenic Philosophy and Evolutionary Biology, 2015
9. *Annambhaṭṭa, Kāśīnātha Pāṇḍuraṅga Paraba, Tarkasangraha* of *Annam Bhatta*, Pg 23
10. Ram Murti Sharma, *Bharatiya darshan ki chintandhara* - Page 283.

CHAPTER FIVE

ALL WORDS CONVEY THE UNIVERSAL

All words convey the universal(as its meaning) and the highest universal is "being". Hence all words convey "Being". Being is identical to "*Brahman*" [1]. Existence is *Brahman* as all we can say about him is "He is" or he is "Existence"[2]. All words hence convey *Brahman*. "Brahman" is the Hindu form of God (Vishnu) as per the religious books [3]. Absolute Existence is called as *Vishnu* (all pervading) as it is in everything and everywhere[4]. Absolute existence is also called as the *Paramatma* or supreme soul[5].

Jati is what remains persistent in all the changes a thing undergoes. For example when you destroy brass bangles, what is left is brass, so brass is the *jati* and the shape of the bangle was the *guna* or quality. So if we keep destroying the object we find that the common universal to all states is "Being/Existence". For the second case too the object will have existence. Hence the highest universal is "being".

Bhartrhari explains that being/reality(*satta*) when it appears in a temporal sequence in particular things is called action/*kriya*/*bhava*. And without any temporal sequence, it is called a thing. Hence a thing and action are two aspects of the same existence seen from the static and dynamic points of view. A thing is static existence/being and action is dynamic existence/being. Both are manifestations of reality [6]. This is depicted in Figure 1.

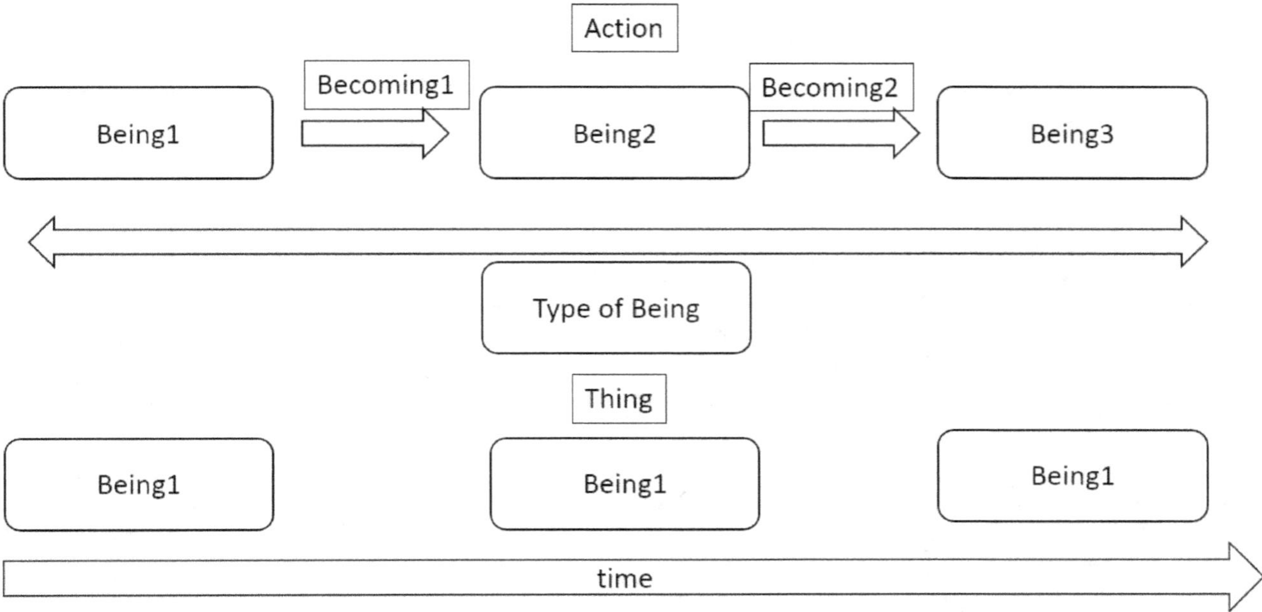

Figure 1. Dynamic Existence: Action and Static Existence: A Thing

Word meaning is the universal or what is indicated by a word is the universal.

Proof:

- **What is a Universal:** Something which exists in all its substrata, as a result of which all of them produce a uniform cognition and are called by the same name.

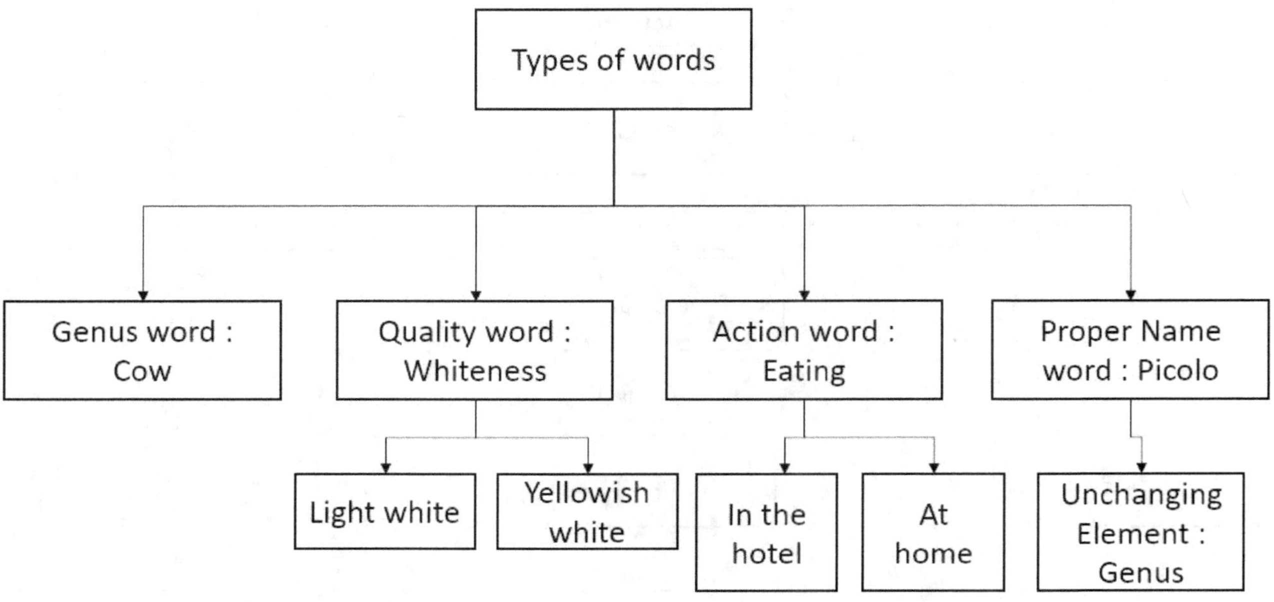

Figure 2. The four classes of words

Classification of words is into four types:

- **Genus word:** The universal/genus consists of all objects belonging to the class. Example: Tree. Genus: All trees.
- **Quality word:** The universal consists in that they distinguish things from other things of a class. So the Genus consists of the things which they distinguish. Example: White. Genus word : All white things. All these things produce the cognition of whiteness.
- **Action word:** The universal/genus consists of all similar actions distinguished by subject, object, position, time etc. Example: Eat. Genus: All Eating actions are separated by qualifiers, space and time. All these actions produce the same cognition of eating.
- **Proper name word:** It stands for that unchanging recognizable element which persists in all the changes which it undergoes. Why this is so is because if an object changes, it still remains the object hence the object is something which persists across the change and which we know to be the genus. Hence the name also denotes the universal. Example: Picolo [7]. The four types of words have been listed in Figure 2. With their respective examples.

So we see that all four kinds of words convey the universal and the highest universal is "Existence/Being" which will be proved in the next chapter.

Notes

1. *Vakyapadiyam* of Bhartrhari, III.1.35 commentary.
2. *Taittiriya Upanishad* – Brahmananda Valli – 2-6.
3. *Vishnu Purana* 1.22.49-51.
4. *Vishnu Purana* 1.2.10-13.
5. *Vishnu Purana* 6.4.37
6. Karl H Potter, *Encyclopedia of Indian philosophies*, Volume V Pg 108.
7. Makkhanalāla Śarmā, *Bhāratīya kāvyaśāstra ke siddhānta* - Page 69.

CHAPTER SIX

"Satta" or "Existence/Being": The Highest Universal

A word conveys universals, the types of words are name word, genus word, quality word and action word. They signify name, genus, quality and action which are universals as discussed before. We visit the universal again:

What is a Universal: Something which exists in all its substrata, as a result of which all of them produce a uniform cognition and are called by the same name.

So a "genus is", "quality is" and "action is". What is implied is that they exist or are existent. They have existence(a universal). Also parallelly genus, name, quality and action are "things" and each of them is basically "how a thing is" or "a type of being" or "being" itself, So we can conclude that the universal of the universals genus, quality and action is "Being" or "Existence", hence Existence is the highest universal as all other universals come under it.

What we see here is that all words represent one of the four universals and these four universals come under existence. The highest universal is existence. As words refer to universals all words refer to Existence.

So the conclusion is that all words (four kinds) refer to the universal "Existence/being". And all words are a type of existence/being(as they belong to that class) or more precisely the universal conveyed by a word is a type of "Existence/Being". This is depicted in Figure 1.

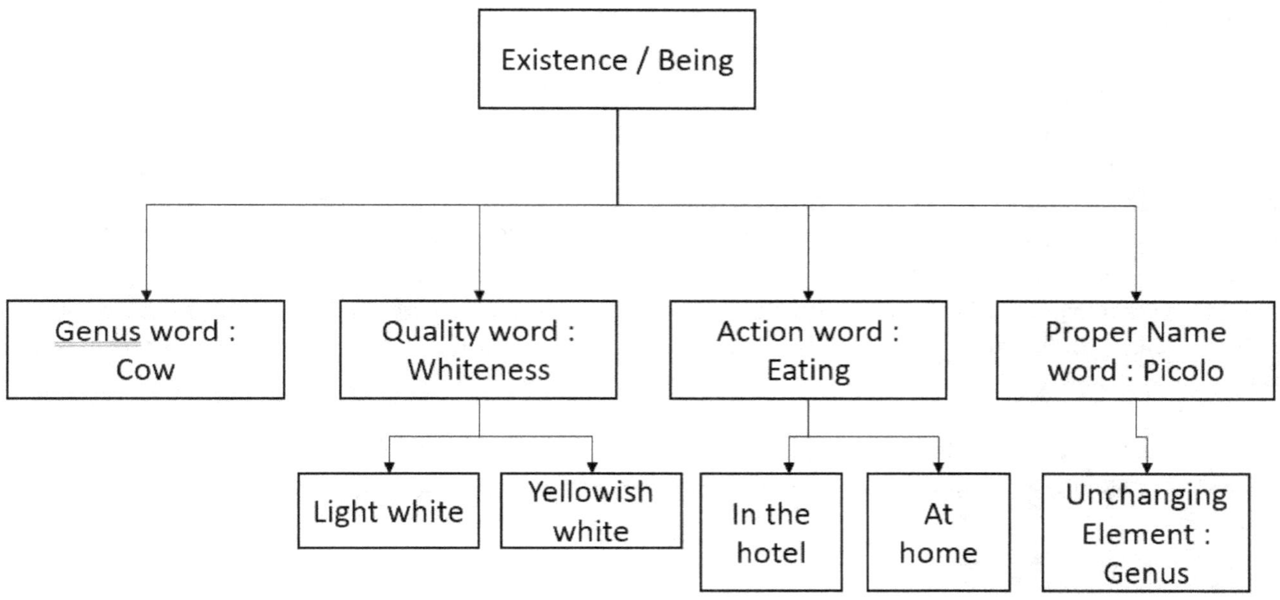

Figure 1. The four classes of words are types of Existence i.e., all fall in the class of Existence.

Significance of all words conveying "Existence/Being":

- This existence or being is called *satta* in Sanskrit. Hence all words convey objects which are manifestations of *satta* ("Existence/Being"). [1]
- All objects are a type of "existence" or "being". They belong to the "absolute existence" genus.
- Existence inheres in all objects as even a non-existent object exists in the mind. Absolute existence pervades all objects and also all objects are a type of it. It is everything and everywhere as well. [2]
- Existence is one only. It is a common characteristic of all entities. It is all-pervading and filling all space, very large in its extent, and it is called *Brahman*.
- That which fills, that which swells, that which expands, that which is everywhere and in all things—That is the completeness, the fullness of Reality; and that is called *Brahman* in the Sanskrit language [3]. All existent things are nothing but a type of existence itself or pure existence hence everything is a type of existence. It sustains or upholds everything as without existence an object cannot be.

Occurrence of "Existence/Being" in religion:

- According to Hinduism the 'satta' (existence) in each and all is God. In Hinduism, it is referred to as *Paramatma* or the supreme spirit [4].
- The all-pervading *satta* ("Being") is referred to as *Vishnu* in the *Puranas* (as it is all-pervading). *Vishnu* is the supreme god of Hinduism [5].
- "In the beginning, this [universe] was "Being/Existence" (*Sat*) alone, one only without a second". He desired, 'I shall become many and be born. He performed *Tapas* (austerities). having performed *Tapas,* He created all this (whatever we perceive). Having created it, He entered into it. Having entered it, He became the manifest and the unmanifest, the defined and undefined, the housed and the houseless, knowledge and ignorance, truth and falsehood, and all this whatsoever that exists. Therefore, it is called Existence', according to a sacred Hindu book [6].
- Existence is all existent and non-existent entities. *Ahimsa* and why to follow it stems from the fact, that he who injures living creatures, injures *Vishnu*(or God): for *Vishnu(Existence)* is all things [7].

Notes

1. *Vakyapadiyam* of Bhartrhari, III.1.35 commentary.
2. *Vakyapadiyam* of Bhartrhari, III.1.34 commentary.
3. https://www.swami-krishnananda.org/upanishad/upan_06.html
4. *Vishnu Purana* 6.4.37
5. *Vishnu Purana* 6.4.37
6. *Taittiriya Upanishad* – Brahmananda Valli – 2-6.
7. *Vishnu Purana* 1.2.10-13

CHAPTER SEVEN

THE PHILOSOPHY OF "ACTION"

Yaska denotes a verb (indicating an action) to denote *bhava, bhava* means "to become" or it signifies "becoming" [1]. This *bhava* or "becoming" has six modes or types [2]. According to him, they are:

1. A thing comes into existence: A thing becoming manifest
2. Exists: Thing becoming itself
3. Changes: Thing becoming modified
4. Grows: Thing becoming larger
5. Decays: Things becoming smaller
6. Ceases to exist: Thing becoming unmanifest

Figure 1. and Figure 2. depict the six forms of becoming or the six types of action.

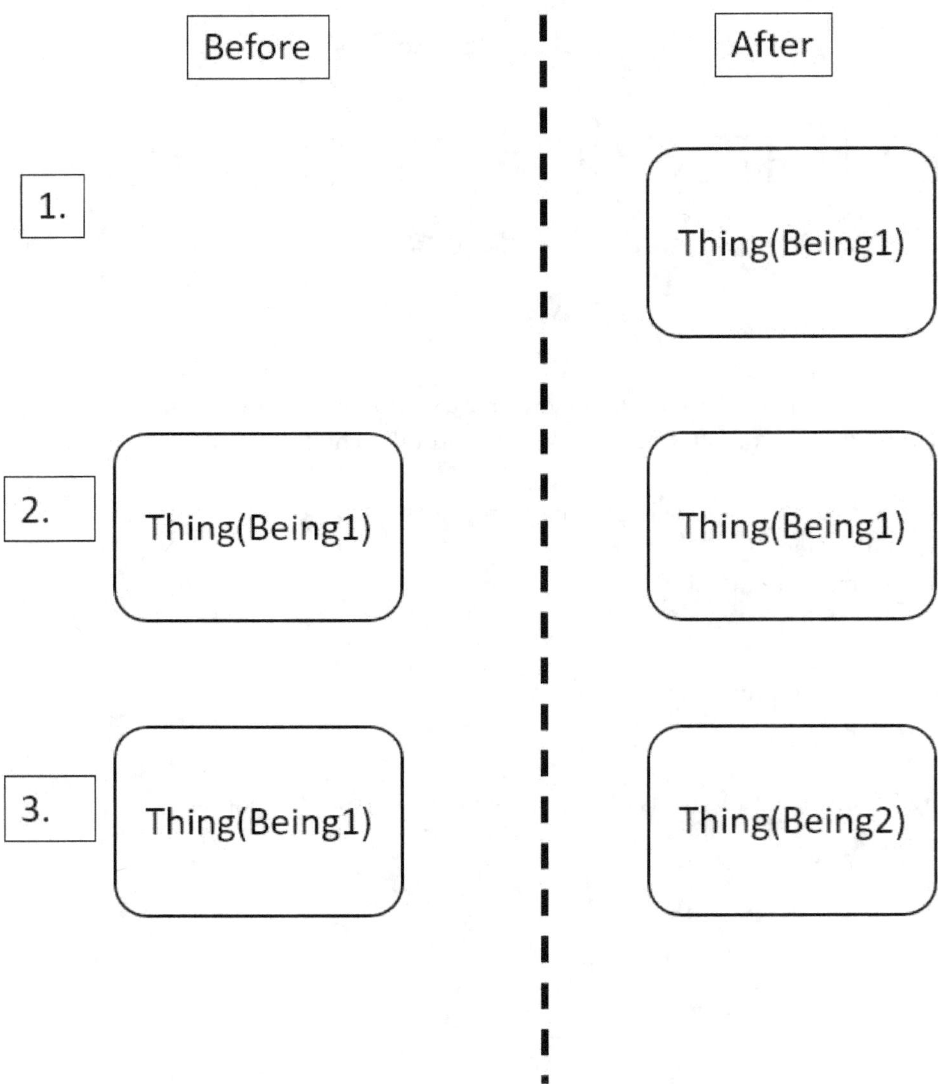

Figure 1. First three types of becoming or action 1. A thing comes into existence, 2. Exists, 3. Changes,

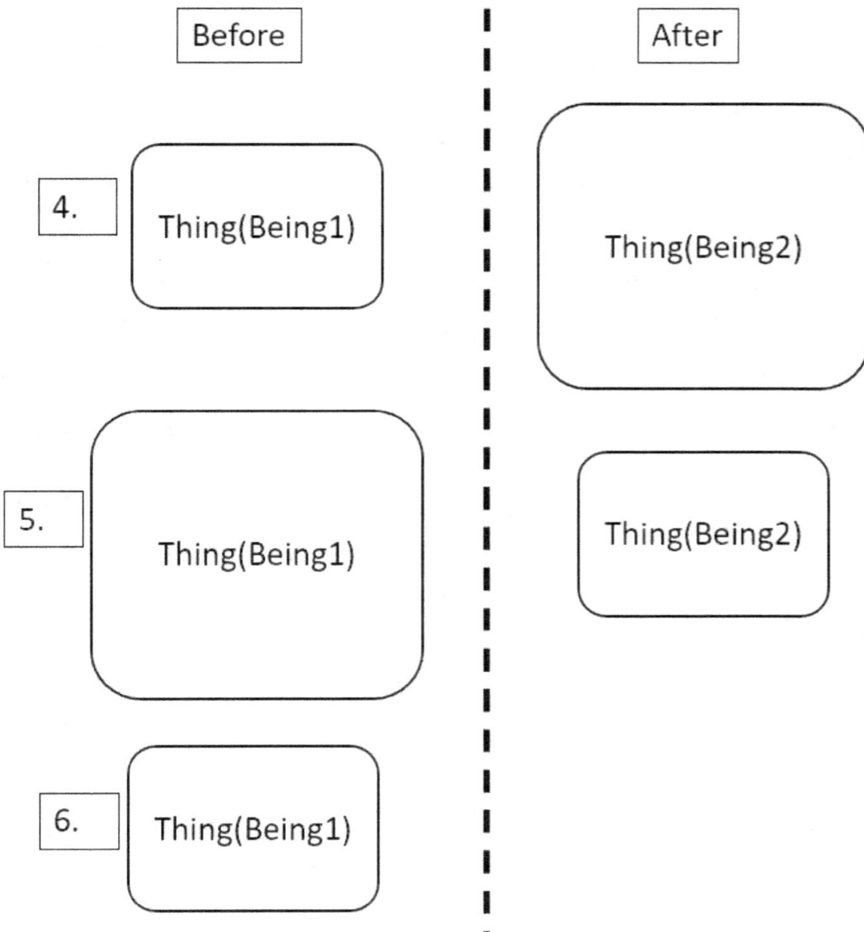

Figure 2. Final three types of becoming or action 4. Grows, 5. Decays, 6. Ceases to exist

Actions can be grouped into six categories: "is born", "exists", "changes", "increases", "decreases" and "is destroyed", these are further divided into "is born", "exists", "is destroyed". Which further fall into the category of "exists"[*asti*] or existence. [3]

All actions fall into a single category called "existence" [*asti*].

Bhartrhari explains that existence, being, reality [*satta*] when it appears in a temporal sequence is called *kriya* or *bhava* or verb [Yaska] and when without temporal sequence it is called *sattva* and is represented by nouns [Yaska]. [4] Figure 3. depicts these concepts.

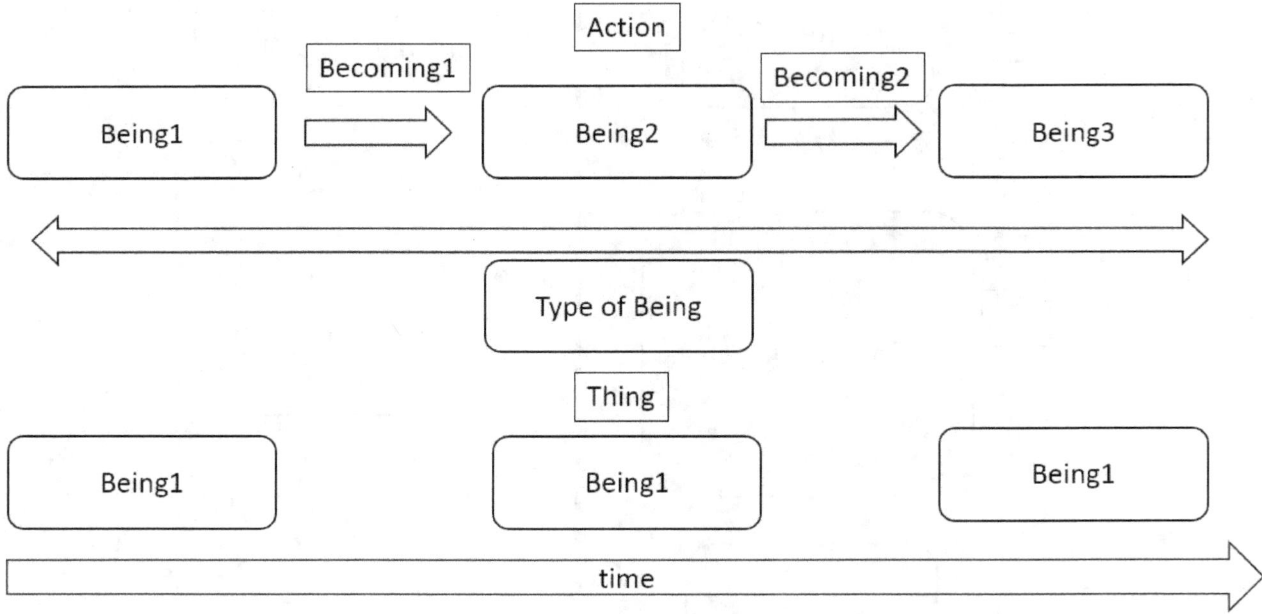

Figure 3. Dynamic Existence: Action(Verb) and Static Existence: A Thing(Noun)

Every object or thing is described by sentences [which indicate action] hence they are a particularization of existence or being.

Generic action again is of two types [5]:

1. Involving movement.
2. Not involving movement but involving a state.

The tradition further divides verbs on the basis of where the action or state is located i.e. in the agent or object/patient [5].

1. Verb where the state is located in the object/patient.
2. Verb where the action is located in the object/patient.
3. Verb where the state is located in the agent.
4. Verb where the action is located in the agent.

The action(*kriya*) is made up of all activities(*vyapara*) whether accomplished or unaccomplished, which are expressed as being accomplished because they have a definite sequence [6]. Figure 4. Depicts this.

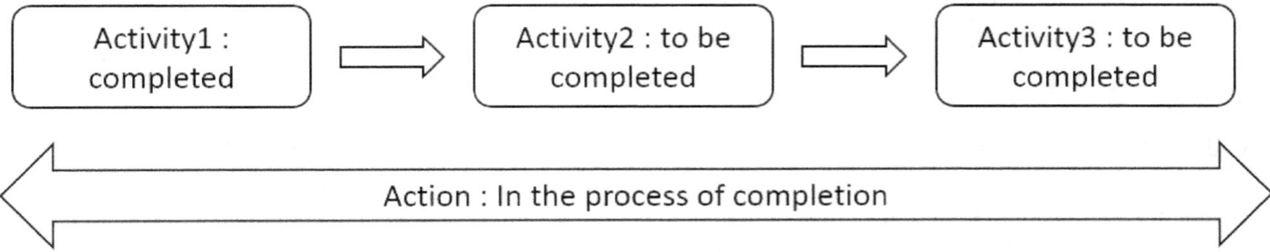

Figure 4. An action composed of activities in the process of completion

An action has both an object of an action (*karma*) as well as the objective of the action, namely the result, that inheres in the object.
The locus of *vyapara* (activity) is the subject.

Two types of sentences are found in language [6][7]:

1. A sentence expressed as something to be accomplished [Action].
2. A sentence expressed as accomplished [Fact].

Sentences of type 2 again can be classified as facts which vary and those that are invariable. **Explanation of the above concepts with examples:**

Who is Krishna

1. Krishna is a person. Accomplished, Genus | Invariable | action type exists
2. Krishna is tall. Accomplished, Quality | Variable | action type exists
3. Krishna eats pasta. Action | in the process of accomplishment | action type, ceases to exist (pasta is eaten or destroyed)
4. Krishna cooks pasta. Action | in the process of accomplishment | a thing comes into existence (pasta)
5. Krishna heats the pasta. Action | in the process of accomplishment | Change: pasta's temperature rises.
6. Krishna increases the fan speed. Action | in the process of accomplishment | Increase
7. Krishna decreases the fan speed. Action | in the process of accomplishment | Decrease
8. Krishna walks. Action | in the process of accomplishment | Movement

Karakas or accomplishers of actions [8]:

Every action has entities which accomplish the action called karakas, they are as follows according to Panini:

1. *Apadana*: The fixed point form which something recedes or departure takes place.
2. *Sampradana*: Indirect object. The entity/ person, whom one wishes to connect with the object (recipient of the object).
3. *Karana*: The most effective means. In English the Instrumental cause.
4. *Adhikararana*: Locus or location where the action takes place.
5. *Karman*: Which is primarily desired by the subject or what the subject seeks most to attain. In English The object/ patient.
6. *Kartr*: The subject/agent.
7. *Hetu*: Which prompts the *kartr* to action or the cause of an action.

To sum up:

Thing : {[S1, S2], S3, S4} : {[A1, A2], A3, A4} : {[c1=> A1,c2 => A2],c3 => A3,c4 =>A4} : existence
Where S1 and S2 are factual sentences and S3, S4 denote action in process of accomplishment.
And A1,A2,A3 and A4 are the respective actions having causes c1, c2, c3 and c4.

Notes:

1. Karl H Potter, *Encyclopedia of Indian philosophies*, Volume V, Pg 107.
2. Karl H Potter, *Encyclopedia of Indian philosophies*, Volume V, Pg 107.
3. Karl H Potter, *Encyclopedia of Indian philosophies*, Volume V, Pg 125.
4. Karl H Potter, *Encyclopedia of Indian philosophies*, Volume V, Pg 108.
5. Edited by Mahendra K. Verma, K. P. Mohanan, *Experiencer Subjects in South Asian Languages*, Madhav M. Deshpande Pg 154.
6. https://semioticon.com/semiotics/cyber/man3.html
7. Edited by Oliver Leaman, *Encyclopedia of Asian Philosophy*, Pg 303
8. R. E. Asher, *The Encyclopedia of Language and Linguistics* Volume 5, Pg 2403

CHAPTER EIGHT

UNIVERSE MODELLING AND THE DIGITAL TWIN

"The universe is the whole of space and all the stars, planets, and other forms of matter and energy in it." [1]

- So a universe for us is defined as A collection of objects which may or may not influence or act upon one another.
- So let's define a universe which consists of objects O1, O2, O3, O4, and O5. U1: {O1, O2, O3, O4, O5}

The objects can have a relation between them of component-whole. O1: whole, O2, and O3 are its components. The relation between O1 and O2, O3 is of inherence. O2 and O3 inhere in O1, so they move together as a whole. U1: {O1[O2, O3], O4, O5}.
Another relation which objects can have amongst themselves is of contact.

So we have the following physical relations amongst objects:

1. Component-Whole
2. Contact
3. Non-contact

These three fundamental physical properties help us visually represent the universe we have defined U1. This Universe can be of any set of objects which influence or act upon one another. The Objects are then modelled as shown in chapter 4.

Objects have the following attributes:

- Name
- Genus
- Qualities
- Actions
- Position in space
- Position in time

Hence we have defined or modelled an object as it occurs.

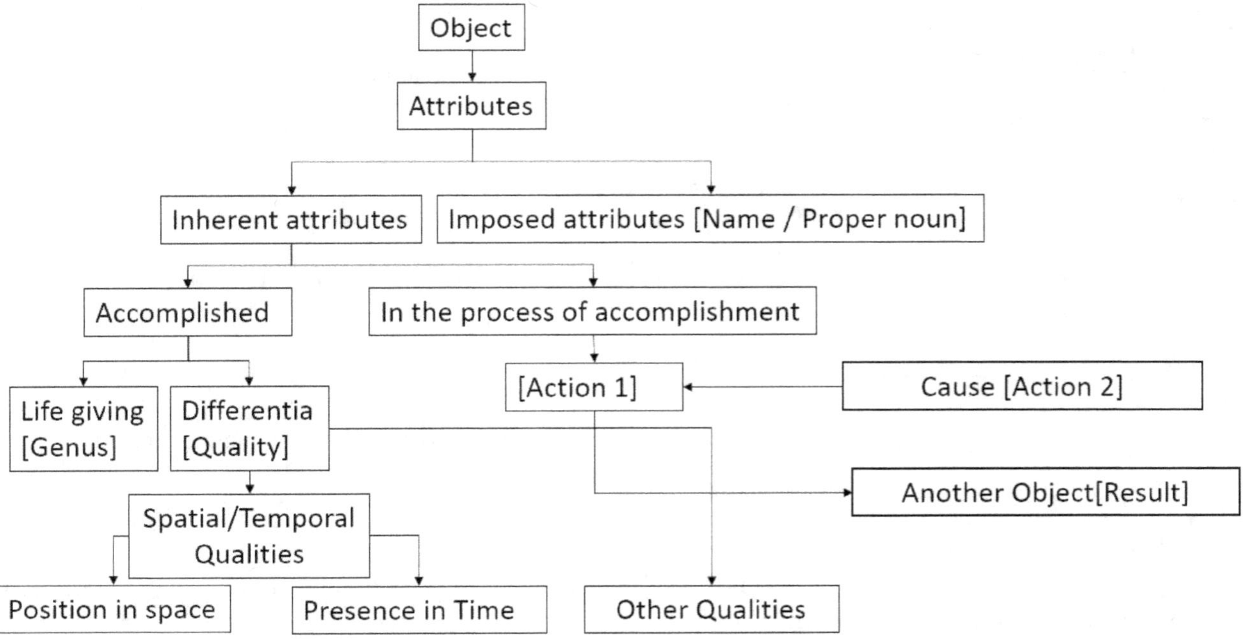

Figure 1. Attributes of an object and how it acts upon another object

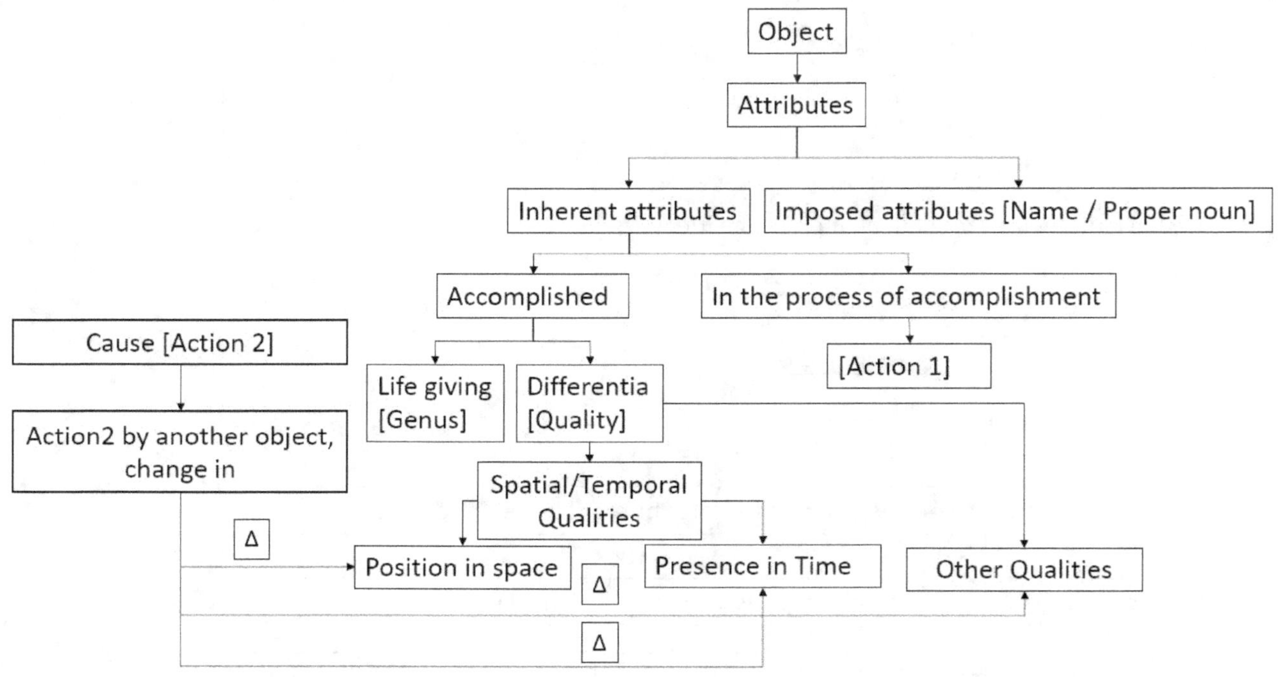

Figure 2. Qualities of an object and how it is changed by another object through its action

Now we bring in the interaction part:
Each Object has actions and the *karaka hetu,* or "cause" in English, which prompts the object to action and the patient/verbal object receives the result of the action.

Action according to Yaska can be one of the following:

1. Object comes into existence
2. Object exists
3. Object changes
4. Object grows
5. Object decays

6. Object ceases to exist
7. And additionally, this might or might not occur Object exhibits movement

And it follows a cause, which would be another action. Hence a control structure occurs as shown in Figure 1 and Figure 2. Figure 1. Depicts how an object acts upon another object and Figure 2. Shows how it receives the action of another object. And the action has a time duration which decides the speed of the action and after that time duration has elapsed the result is reflected in the action receiving object.

Also, these objects have spatial positions and presence in time.

Hence a universe has been modelled. The advantage of this universe modelling is that it can be applied to imperceptible objects too and hence extends to domains like economics and other fields of science which are imperceptible. This modelling is universal and applies to all fields of science and study.

The Digital Twin:
A Digital Twin is a virtual representation that is the real-time digital analogue of a physical object or process [2]. The universe which we modelled above can be used as a model and real-time data fed which leads to the perfect replication of the physical system or universe. The ontology provided by the Sanskrit language has brought clarity to the Digital Twin design process and simplified a very complex task to the fundamentals of the language.

Sample Universe experiments:
A sample Universe consisting of a woodcutter, tree and a factory was constructed in Python Language. Where the woodcutter cuts trees and collects wood and stores it in the factory. The whole Universe was coded in 1000 lines with the possibility to expand through config files. Figure 3. shows a screenshot of the sample Universe. Such compact Universes can be built for any application or field of study. If they take sensor inputs they would behave as a digital replica of a real-world system.

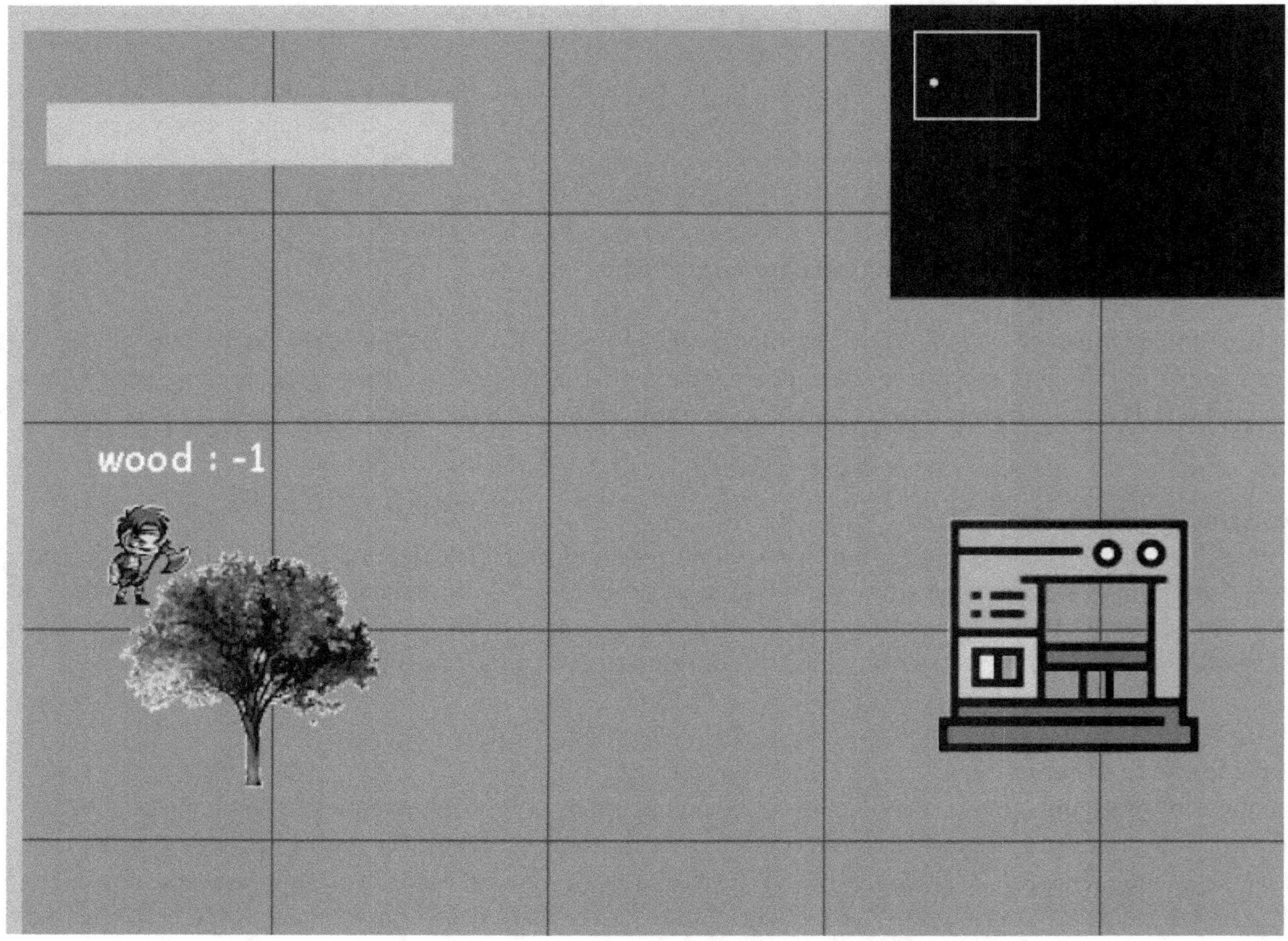

Figure 3. A sample Universe consisting of a woodcutter, tree and a factory

Conclusion:

The methodologies for creating a universe and a Digital Twin have been shared which are based on the Sanskrit language and are explained in a way which can be used to make digital twins or universes for any field of science and study in the English language. This kind of modelling removes the clutter of language and reduces an object to basic entities like genus, quality and action which streamlines knowledge and the thought process that follows. Hence imparts clarity and refines that field of science or study. Giving something which is so complex (various fields of science) a systematic and procedural structure.

Science, as we know it now, is like a forest, beautiful and complex and with the theory presented in this work it can be made simple, efficient and structured like a city giving it endless possibilities for growth. This work is applicable to all fields of studies like Economics, Medicine, Geology, Law etc which involve a "Universe" of objects.

Notes

1. COBUILD Advanced English Dictionary. Copyright © HarperCollins Publishers.
2. https://en.wikipedia.org/wiki/Digital_twin

Non-Technical Applications of the Linguistic Theorems

One's true scientific identity, oneness with all living creatures and the theory of *Karma*

CHAPTER NINE

APPLICATION OF IDENTITY THEOREM: OUR TRUE IDENTITY AND WHY ALL LIVING BEINGS ARE ONE

Identity theorem: An object stands for that unchanging recognizable element which persists in all the changes which it undergoes [1]. Why this is so because if an object changes, it still remains the object; hence the object is something which persists across the change and which we know to be the genus or universal. This unchanging recognizable element persists, as a result, we are able to identify the object across all changes. Figure 1 depicts this.

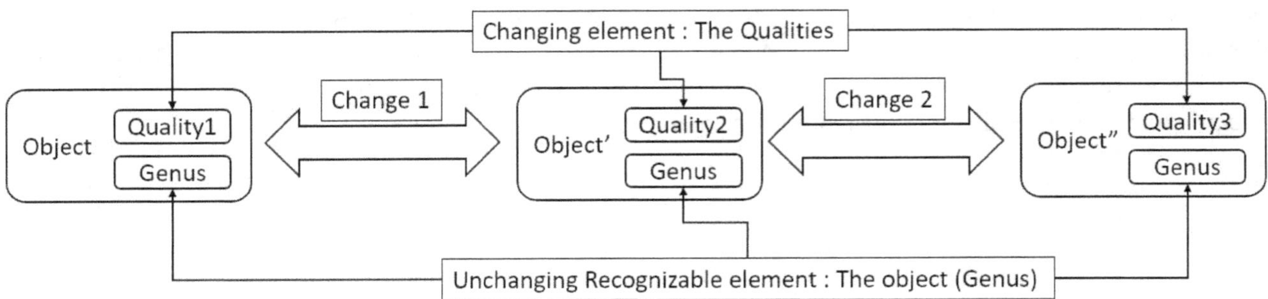

Figure 1. While an object undergoes changes, the identity is the "unchanging"; the unchanging is the reason for us recognizing the object or it still being the object.

To start with let us assume that you are the body and the consciousness.

i.e., you are: Body + consciousness

Everything about the body is changeable and it is continuously changing from birth to death. What we perceive as the body is something which continuously undergoes biological changes. Rather the body evolves and grows through changes, which is a fundamental aspect of life. Further, the constitution of organs is never constant, it is subject to growth/decay.

Let us say an individual by the name of *Shyam* remains the same person and does not become someone else despite all changes. In spite of all biological changes in *Shyam* from birth to death, there exists a constant element which is the identity of *Shyam*. And this identity cannot be the body as the body undergoes changes.

So is the identity "consciousness"?

Our consciousness remains unchanged from birth to death. It is consciousness which makes us aware of the world. Through the senses and we experience pleasure and pain, brought about by the contact of the objects of the senses with the senses viz. tongue, eyes, ears, nose and skin and mind.

Our consciousness persists across all changes, when we are awake, when we are asleep or when we dream. When we are awake we experience the world. When we are asleep we experience rest or bliss. When we dream we experience a series of thoughts, images, and sensations. When one is no more his identity is lost and so is his consciousness, while the body remains till it disappears. Death brings loss of functioning of the body as well which is due to the fact that the person is no more alive or conscious. Consciousness enlivens the body.

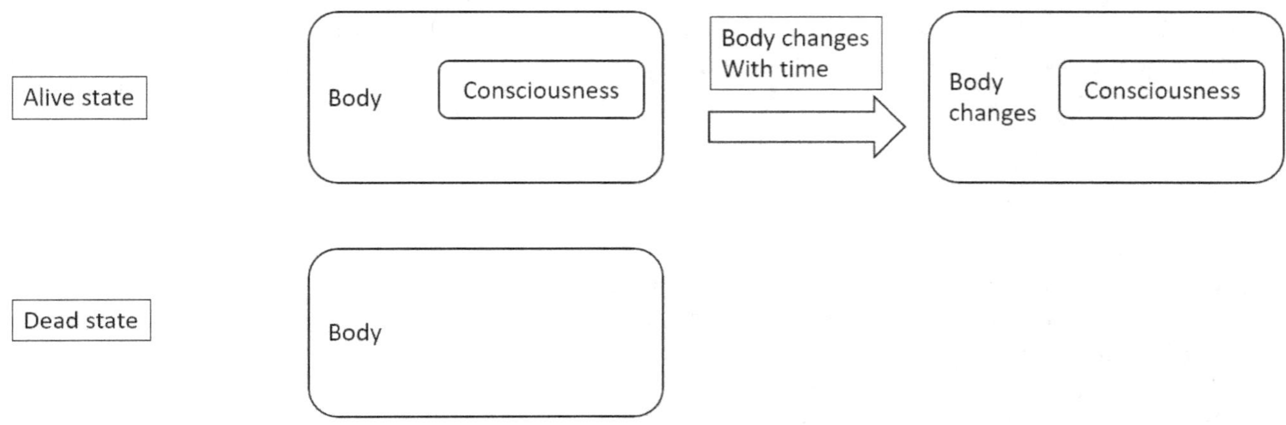

Figure 2. Body and consciousness, when alive and dead

Figure 2 depicts that consciousness persists till the person is dead. When the person is no more consciousness is lost; hence it is only consciousness that is the identity of a person. This analysis is applicable to all living creatures. Our identity is one which unites us. Hence we are one. We should not injure another living creature or hurt it as we would be hurting only ourselves, our consciousness. This has given rise to the concept of non-violence (*Ahimsa*) towards all. This thought process is along the same lines of thought of Mahatma Gandhi, who held the view that without truth and nonviolence there can be nothing but the destruction of humanity. Mahatma Gandhi said that "the realization of the truth which is the realization of the oneness with all that is created as an extension of oneself portrays *ahimsa.*" [2] This work strengthens that concept.

The configuration of the body and self as per the *Upanishad* (an Indian religious book) is as follows:
"Know the Self to be sitting in the chariot, the body to be the chariot, the intellect (buddhi) the charioteer, and the mind (the inner instrument, or inner organ of thought and feeling) the reins. The senses (tongue, eyes, ears, nose and skin) they call the horses, the objects of the senses their roads. When He (the Highest Self) is in union with the body, the senses, and the mind, then wise people call him the Enjoyer" [3].

As per the *Mahabharata* (an Indian religious book):

"The senses exist for simply seizing the impressions of their respective objects. The Mind has doubt for its function. The Understanding (*Buddhi*, intellect) is for ascertainment. The soul is said to be only an inactive witness (of the functions of the others). The senses are for perceiving; the mind (unable to deal with those perceptions) produces uncertainty. The understanding reduces all perceptions to certainty. The Soul exists as a witness (without acting)" [4].

Notes

1. *Vakyapadiyam* of Bhartrhari, III.1.11, III.1.12 commentary.
2. Ahimsa: Its theory and practice in Gandhism | Peace, Nonviolence & Conflict Resolution | Articles on and by Mahatma Gandhi (mkgandhi.org)
   https://www.mkgandhi.org/articles/ahimsa-Its-theory-and-practice-in-Gandhism.html
3. Max Müller, *The Upanishads*, Part 2 (SBE15), 3.3, 3.4, 3.5
4. Kisari Mohan Ganguli, *The Mahabharata* Book 12: *Santi Parva, Mokshadharma Parva*: Section CCLXXXVI

CHAPTER TEN

DESIRES, THE PURSUIT OF HAPPINESS, ACTION AND THE CONSEQUENCES OF ACTION

Why do we act at all?

All acts have for their purpose the attainment of happiness [1]. Hence we act to attain happiness by the fulfilment of the desire or goal. There are two kinds of consequences in respect of our acts, the springing of happiness from good acts and sorrow from sinful, acts [2] which we will prove in the coming sections.

Karma Theorem :

The cause of action in Indian philosophy is desire [3], and the cause of desire is "lack" or a "sense of limitation" [4]. _Karma_ means the actions and deeds that we perform. Having mentally chosen a goal a person acts, the results of the action are either success in obtaining the goal or failure this purely depends partly on our effort, partly on our fate and partly on our luck, but with the dint of our effort we can bring success [5]. The results of our action are not pre-decided, nor are they random nor are they completely under our control, it is the sum of the above-discussed factors. Apart from this immediate result is the consequences of an action which acts upon us immediately or in the future. The consequences of action on us are called _karmaphala_ which is Happiness(reward) for good actions or suffering(punishment) for bad actions [6][7]. But crimes (bad acts) should not be confused with punishment as both are on the opposite spectrum of acts, punishment is given for committing a crime (bad acts) and not vice versa. So all our actions have consequences which affect us and form our future or fate. Fate is a result of past activities and it consists of the consequences of our past actions consisting of rewards and punishments, bringing happiness or suffering [8].

Actions we commit are of two types: good actions(*dharma*) and bad actions(*adharma*). Acts of kindness are good acts and are called *dharma* (virtue) [9]. Acts which cause pain to others are called *adharma* (vice). *Adharma* destroys the world and *dharma* sustains the world as one is an act of kindness or goodness and the other is an act of injury which destroys. The consequences of our good actions are rewards(happiness) and the consequence of bad actions are punishments(suffering) [8].

Hence The *Karma* theorem is that good actions have pleasure as their consequence and bad actions have pain as their consequence (which fall upon us). The pain comes as a result of bad action and is a check on it and the pleasure as a result of good action is a stimulus or incentive to do further good actions.[6][7]

Proof :

1. So let us first prove that our actions have a consequence on us. The consequences of *Karma* could be as simple as just feeling good from kind acts and feeling bad or guilty from hurting a living creature. If actions had no consequence (i.e. fruitless) being inconsequential they wouldn't produce happiness or sorrow. Everything would be of no avail as acts would not give happiness or suffering (the very motivators and demotivators of an act) and hence no one would perform any acts and be idlers and depending on destiny the world would be neutralized [10].
2. Hence acts are consequential.
3. Let us assume the consequences of good acts are good experiences or happiness and the consequences of bad acts are bad experiences or suffering, which acts as a punishment for bad acts and reward for good acts. Punishments cause people to refrain from bad actions and take up good actions and stimulus/incentive for good actions, causes people to perform good actions (an incentive also causes a change of behaviour [11] and here it encourages us to do good actions). Hence bad actions would be limited and discouraged and people would be encouraged to take up good acts and the world would be sustained. So a system of checks and stimuli is required to run and sustain the world.
4. And if the polarity of consequence was also reversed i.e. suffering(punishment) for good actions and happiness (reward) for bad actions then again bad actions would be followed and the world would be neutralized.
5. As all the contrary scenarios to the theory of *Karma* are not observed hence the above-mentioned situations do not occur. Actions being consequential and a source of happiness is what motivates us to act and this system of punishment and reward is what sustains the world. So the existence of the *Karma* system is proved.
6. If fate purely depended on chance or luck, the world would be neutralized or in chaos.

The stimulus for good acts :
Feeling Good (happiness) as a result of the good act and good experiences in the future.

Punishment/Check for bad acts :
Feeling bad (suffering) as a result of the bad act and bad experiences in the future.

A. Actions: Good and Bad, without consequences:
Consequences: None
Scenario: Actions being inconsequential produce no happiness or suffering, providing no motivation for acting, hence all become idlers and people depend on Chance => World is neutralized

B. Actions: Good and Bad, with consequences:
Consequences : Good experiences [Reward : Happiness] and Bad experiences [Punishment : suffering]
Action => Consequences/fate
So for the good and bad actions, there will be consequences. By good actions, the world is sustained and by bad actions the world is destroyed.

Let's see the combination of actions and consequences.

1. Good actions =>
Consequences [good] – people repeat good actions as the incentive is pleasure and hence the world is sustained.
Consequences [bad] – people don't adhere to good actions and resort to bad actions and the world is destroyed.

2. Bad actions =>
Consequences [good] – people repeat bad actions and the world is destroyed.
Consequences [bad] – people don't adhere to bad actions as they are punished for it and the world is sustained.

C. The third scenario
The third scenario could be that the consequence is by chance or random, if it was by chance the world would be different from one moment to another and destroyed.

Karmaphala, the Check and stimulus system:

Here bad acts are shunned as they incur punishment and cause pain. And good acts are performed as they result in rewards which produce pleasure.

To sum it up: Happiness comes due to good actions, and suffering results from bad actions. Hence the law of *Karma* is proved.

How to decide what is a good act and what is a bad act:
One should never do that to another which one regards as injurious/unpleasant to one's own self. This, in brief, is the rule of righteousness or what is a good act and the converse is a bad act [9]. For example someone is allergic to something and you knowingly give the allergen, its a bad act as this act causes pain to the recipient. Also to judge it as bad if you were in their shoes and you were given the allergen you would experience pain and label the action as bad. This is how you judge what act is good and what act is bad. A man of good actions becomes good by those actions and a man of bad actions bad by those actions[12]. To sum it up: In happiness and misery, in the agreeable and the disagreeable, one should judge effects as if they came to one's own self. And then deem it as good or bad [13]. One should not judge an act as a witness but as a recipient (placing themselves in the recipient's shoes).

Some immediate fruits of one's action:
The immediate consequence of hurting someone or performing an act of kindness is discussed here. "When one injures another, the injured turns round and injures the injurer. Similarly, when one cherishes another, that other cherishes the cherisher. One should frame one's rule of conduct according to this. I have told thee what righteousness is even by this subtle way." [13]

"That man who keeps under control the three faults, viz., lust, wrath, and cupidity, by throwing them upon all creatures (and practises the virtue of compassion), attains success"[13].

"That man who regards all creatures as his own self, and behaves towards them as towards his own self, laying aside the rod of chastisement and completely subjugating his wrath, succeeds in attaining happiness" [13].

"One should never do that to another which one regards as injurious to one's own self. This, in brief, is the rule of Righteousness. One by acting in a different way by yielding to desire becomes guilty of unrighteousness" [9].

***Adharma* and *dharma* or good acts and bad acts (according to *Vatsayana*, a 4th-century Hindu scholar)[14][15]:**

***Adharma* (vice) of body:**

1. *Hinsa* (violence),

2. *Steya* (steal, theft),
3. *Pratisiddha maithuna* (sexual indulgence with someone other than one's marital partner). Marriage here implies a marriage between a man and a woman and is according to the Hindu religion.

Dharma (virtue) of body:

1. *Dana* (charity),
2. *Paritrana* (succor of the distressed) and
3. *Paricarana* (rendering service to others)

Adharma (vice) of mind:

1. *Paradroha* (ill will to anyone),
2. *Paradravyabhipsa* (covetousness),
3. *Nastikya* (denial of the existence of morals and religiosity)

Dharma (virtue) of mind:

1. *Daya* (compassion),
2. *Asprha* (disinterestedness), and
3. *Sraddha* (faith in other people)

Adharma (vice) from words one speaks or writes:

1. *Mithya* (falsehood),
2. *Parusa* (caustic talk),
3. *Sucana* (calumny) and
4. *Asambaddha* (absurd talk)

Dharma (virtue) from words one speaks or writes:

1. *Satya* (truth and facts),
2. *Hitavacana* (talking with good intention),
3. *Priyavacana* (gentle, kind talk),
4. *Svadhyaya* (self-study)

We have already discussed that some actions are *adharma* or bad acts as they cause injury and the remaining actions *dharma* or good acts as they are acts of kindness. And by the laws of *Karma* good acts are rewarded and bad acts are punished.

The Pursuit of Happiness:

Happiness is the result of good conduct (*dharma*) [16], good conduct is defined in *Mahabharata* as "abstention from injury, by act, thought, and word, in respect of all creatures, compassion, and gift, constitute behavior that is worthy of praise (good conduct). That act or exertion by which others are not benefited, or that act in consequence of which one must feel shame, should never be done. That act, on the other hand, should be done in consequence of which one may win praise in society" [17].

Notes:

1. Kisari Mohan Ganguli, The Mahabharata Book 12: Santi Parva SECTION CXC
2. Kisari Mohan Ganguli, Mahabharata SECTION, Book 12: Santi Parva, CXC
3. Śaṅkara, Select Works of Sri Sankaracharya: Sanskrit Text and English Translation, Direct Realisation, verse 14
4. Paul Bahder, Carol Bahder, Be Free From "Me": Vedanta Notes. Chapter 19
5. Draupadi on Fate, https://arshabodha.org/wp-content/uploads/abc/teachings/articles/Draupadi_on_Fate.pdf
6. Source: DDSA: The practical Sanskrit-English dictionary
7. Mahabharata, xiii.6.10 & 19
8. Adṛṣṭa, Source: DDSA: The practical Sanskrit-English dictionary
9. Brihaspati, Mahabharata 13.113.8
10. Kisari Mohan Ganguli, The Mahabharata, Book 13: Anusasana Parva SECTION VI
11. Incentive, Definition from Oxford Languages
12. Brihadaranyaka Upanishad IV, 4, 5
13. Mahabharata; book 13: Anusasana Parva, Section 113
14. Klaus Klostermaier, A survey of Hinduism, SUNY Press, ISBN 0-88706-807-3, Chapter 3: "Hindu dharma".

15. Jha, Nyayasutras with Vatsyayana Bhasya, 2 vols, Oriental Books (1939).
16. Ashtangarhudaya, Sutrasthan, Adhyaya 2, Shloka 19
17. Kisari Mohan Ganguli, The Mahabharata, Book 13: Rajadharmanusasana Parva: Section CXXIV

CHAPTER ELEVEN

THE LOGICAL WAYS OF LIFE THAT FOLLOW FROM THE PHILOSOPHY DISCUSSED

1. Our identity is "consciousness" and so is it the identity of all living beings, hence we are "One". [chapter 9]
2. We are one and therefore follow the concept of non-injury (*Ahimsa*) towards all. As one would be only hurting oneself by hurting another. Also the concept of "another" disappears in this world. [chapter 9]
3. "Absolute Existence" or "*Sat*" is revered by the Hindus as God (*Brahman, Vishnu*). Everything is a type of or manifestation of this existence and in everything this "Existence" inheres, making it very sacred. As it inheres in everything and everywhere it is called *Paramatma* or Supreme spirit by the Hindus. [chapter 6]
4. As everyone houses this sacred spirit, everyone is sacred and hence must be revered, cherished and respected. [chapter 6]
5. As all are one, the right action is to treat all equally like own with love, respect and affection. All beings are the manifestation of "Absolute existence", which is everywhere and in everything. [chapter 6]
6. For every action there is an equal and opposite reaction i.e. our actions bear consequences. [chapter 10]
7. Happiness comes due to good actions and suffering results from bad actions. [chapter 10]